Sacagawea

Jennifer Strand

abdopublishing.com

Published by Abdo Zoom™, PO Box 398166, Minneapolis, Minnesota 55439. Copyright © 2018 by Abdo Consulting Group, Inc. International copyrights reserved in all countries. No part of this book may be reproduced in any form without written permission from the publisher. Abdo Zoom™ is a trademark and logo of Abdo Consulting Group, Inc.

Printed in the United States of America, North Mankato, Minnesota
052017
092017

THIS BOOK CONTAINS
RECYCLED MATERIALS

Cover Photo: Todd Strand/Independent Picture Service/Alamy
Interior Photos: Todd Strand/Independent Picture Service/Alamy, 1; Everett Historical/Shutterstock Images, 4–5, 10 (left), 10 (right), 14, 16; Shutterstock Images, 5; Julie Lubick/Shutterstock Images, 6–7; Jerry Hopman/iStockphoto, 8–9; North Wind Photo Archive, 9, 18; Steve Estvanik/Shutterstock Images, 11; iStockphoto, 12–13, 15, 16–17, 19; Nancy Carter/North Wind Photo Archive, 13

Editor: Emily Temple
Series Designer: Madeline Berger
Art Direction: Dorothy Toth

Publisher's Cataloging-in-Publication Data
Names: Strand, Jennifer, author.
Title: Sacagawea / by Jennifer Strand.
Description: Minneapolis, MN : Abdo Zoom, 2018. | Series: Native American leaders | Includes bibliographical references and index.
Identifiers: LCCN 2017931232 | ISBN 9781532120251 (lib. bdg.) | ISBN 9781614797364 (ebook) | 9781614797920 (Read-to-me ebook)
Subjects: LCSH: Sacagawea--Juvenile literature. | Shoshoni women--Biography--Juvenile literature. | Shoshoni Indians--Biography--Juvenile literature. | Lewis and Clark Expedition (1804-1806)--Juvenile literature.
Classification: DDC 978.00497/45740/092 [B]--dc23
LC record available at http://lccn.loc.gov/2017931232

Table of Contents

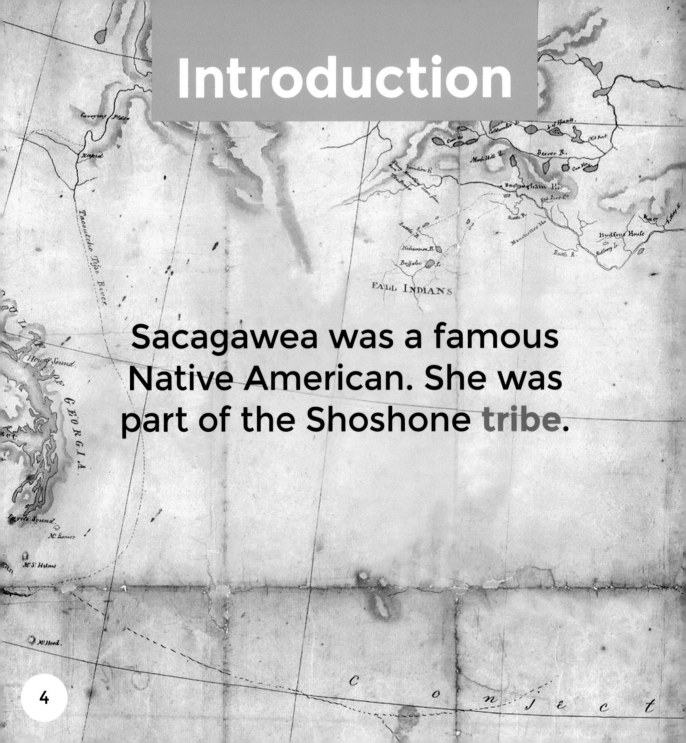

Introduction

Sacagawea was a famous Native American. She was part of the Shoshone **tribe**.

Sacagawea helped
Meriwether Lewis and William Clark
explore the American West.

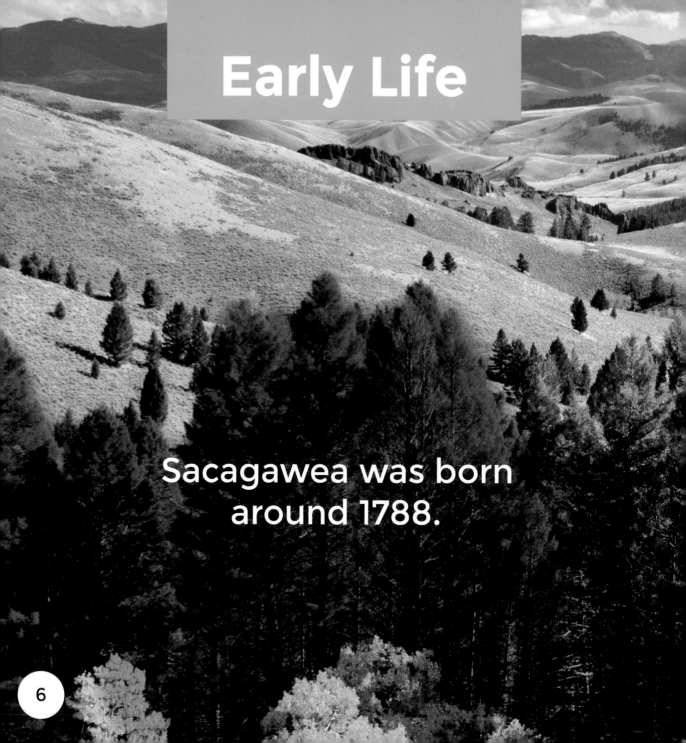

Early Life

Sacagawea was born around 1788.

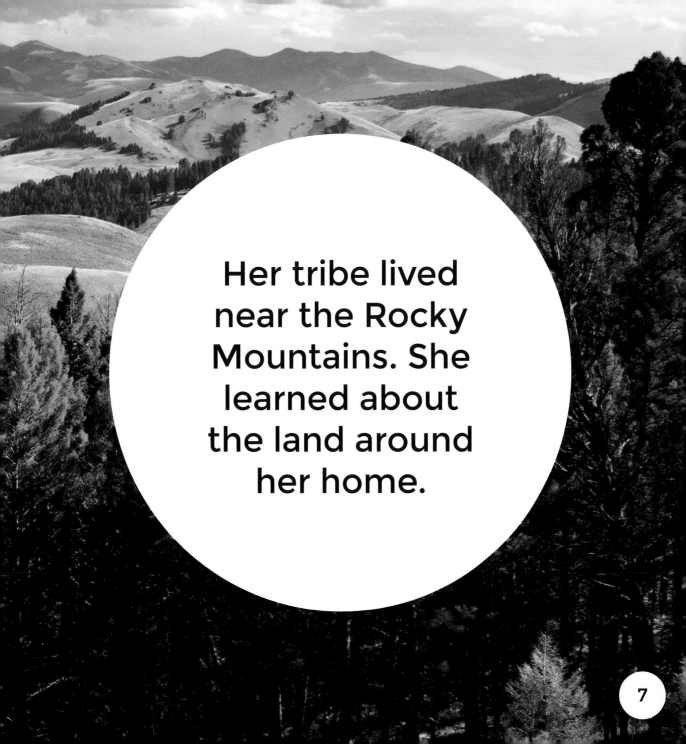

Her tribe lived near the Rocky Mountains. She learned about the land around her home.

Another tribe captured Sacagawea
when she was about 12.
They moved her far away to
a new village.

Later she married a
Canadian fur trader.

Lewis and Clark were **explorers** from the United States.

Their group built a fort.
It was near Sacagawea's new
village. They met Sacagawea
and her husband there.

Lewis and Clark planned to travel west. They needed an **interpreter**. They hired Sacagawea's husband.

But only Sacagawea could speak the Shoshone language. So she came, too.

Sacagawea **translated** for the explorers.

The group met with other Native American tribes. Sacagawea helped everyone get along.

The explorers needed supplies. Sacagawea helped them trade with local tribes.

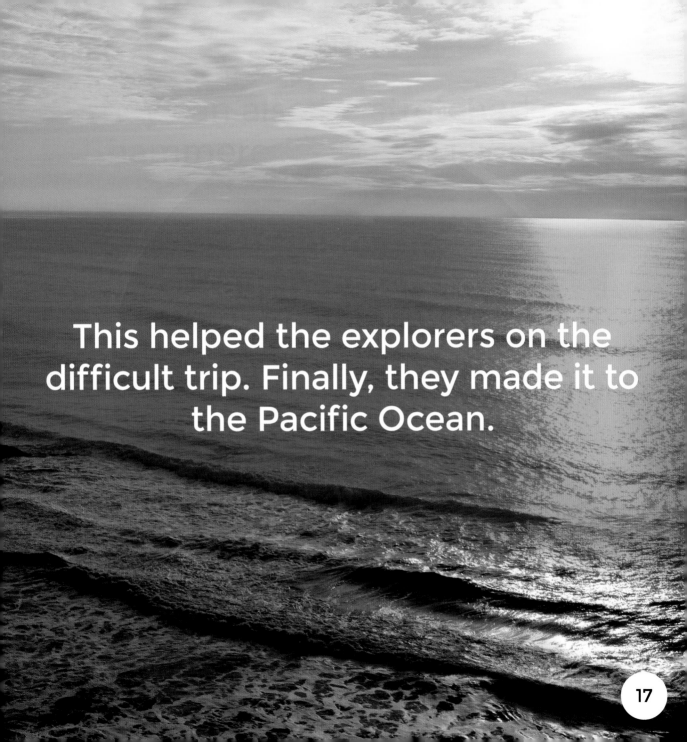

This helped the explorers on the difficult trip. Finally, they made it to the Pacific Ocean.

Sacagawea returned to her village. Lewis and Clark wrote about her.

Sacagawea helped the group learn a lot about the West. She died on December 20, 1812.

Sacagawea

Born: around 1788, the exact date is not known

Birthplace: near modern-day Lemhi, Idaho

Husband: Toussaint Charbonneau

Known For: Sacagawea was a Shoshone woman who helped Meriwether Lewis and William Clark explore the American West.

Died: December 20, 1812

1788: Sacagawea is born around this time. No one knows the exact date.

1800: Another tribe captures Sacagawea and takes her to a village in North Dakota.

1804: Meriwether Lewis and William Clark meet Sacagawea.

1805-1806: Sacagawea joins Lewis and Clark. Their group explores the western United States.

1812: Sacagawea dies on December 20.

Glossary

explorer - a person who travels to new places.

fort - a structure built to survive enemy attacks.

interpreter - a person who changes words between languages.

trader - a person whose job is to buy and sell goods.

translate - to change the words of one language into those of another.

tribe - a group of people who share the same culture and beliefs.

Booklinks

For more information on **Sacagawea**, please visit abdobooklinks.com

 In on Biographies!

Learn even more with the Abdo Zoom Biographies database. Check out **abdozoom.com** for more information.

Index